Negotiating Survival

Four Priorities After Rio

Negotiating Survival
Four Priorities After Rio

Richard N. Gardner

COUNCIL ON FOREIGN RELATIONS PRESS

NEW YORK

COUNCIL ON FOREIGN RELATIONS

Copyright © 1992 by the Council on Foreign Relations, Inc. All rights reserved.
Printed in the United States of America.
ISBN 0-87609-141-9

Library of Congress Cataloguing-in-Publication Data

Gardner, Richard N.
  Negotiating survival : four priorities after Rio / Richard N. Gardner.
    p.   cm. --
  Includes bibliographical references.
  ISBN 0-87609-141-9 : $10.95
  1. United Nations Conference on Environment and Development (1992 : Rio de Janeiro, Brazil) 2. Economic development--Environmental aspects. 3. Environmental policy--International cooperation. 4. Environmental law, International. 5. Population policy. 6. Economic assistance. I. Title.
HD75.6.G38 1992   92-32956
333.7'2--dc20   CIP

---

92 93 94 95 96 97   EB   10   9   8   7   6   5   4   3   2   1

Cover Design by Whit Vye

CONTENTS

1
INTRODUCTION

The United Nations Conference on Environment and Development (UNCED) held in Rio de Janeiro from June 3 to June 14, 1992, otherwise known as the Rio Earth Summit, has launched the world into a new era of eco-diplomacy, eco-negotiation and eco-lawmaking. It was the largest international conference ever held, with over 100 heads of state or government in attendance, 8,000 delegates, 9,000 members of the press, and 3,000 accredited representatives of nongovernmental organizations (NGOs). But what really happened at this "mother of all international conferences"? And what will the decisions made there mean for the future?

The Earth Summit approved three documents—the Rio Declaration on Environment and Development (a collection of twenty-seven nonbinding principles); a nonbinding statement of principles on the management of forests; and Agenda 21, a comprehensive action plan on sustainable development to guide the policies of governments for the remainder of this century and into the next. The Earth Summit also provided the occasion for the signing of two international treaties—the United Nations Framework Convention on Climate Change and the Convention on Biological Di-

1

versity—treaties that had been drafted in separate negotiations that paralleled the Rio preparatory process.

Although one would hardly have known it from the press, it was the Agenda 21 action plan that was the central business of the Rio conference. Its forty chapters, with 115 program areas in over 400 pages of text, covered the whole range of environment and development issues—from atmosphere, soil, forests, and oceans to population, consumption, toxic and solid waste disposal, technology transfer, and financing. The program areas in each chapter were described in terms of basis for action (a definition of the problem), objectives, activities to be undertaken, and means of implementation, including funding requirements. The purpose of Agenda 21 was to forge a global partnership between developed and developing countries in "sustainable development"—defined in 1987 by the World Commission on Environment and Development chaired by Prime Minister Gro Harlem Bruntland of Norway as development that "meets the needs of the present without compromising the ability of future generations to meet their own needs."

The Rio meeting, of course, was not the first global conference to deal with environmental issues. The UN Conference on the Human Environment held at Stockholm twenty years earlier had also adopted an action plan and a Declaration of Principles. Its institutional creation—the United Nations Environment Program (UNEP) in Nairobi—could point to important achievements despite its modest budget and the lack of high-level commitment from governments. UNEP established a global monitoring network as part of a broad assessment program, known as Earthwatch, to provide scientific information on changes in the global environment; stimulated governments to clean up the Mediterranean and other regional seas; helped developing countries train professionals, draft laws, and build institutions for environmental protection; and generally tried to coordinate the family of UN agencies in their support of environmental programs. Perhaps UNEP's greatest achievement was in stimulating and guiding to completion the Vienna Convention for the Protection of the Ozone Layer and its Montreal Protocol.

Yet the Stockholm conference could not be said to have fulfilled its purpose. Between 1972 and 1992, the world's forests grew smaller, its deserts larger, its crop soil thinner. The number of plant and animal species diminished dramatically. And a new threat to global habitability emerged that was only dimly perceived at Stockholm—the danger that increasing emissions of carbon dioxide and other greenhouse gasses could produce significant and possibly catastrophic changes in global climate. According to the Intergovernmental Panel on Climate Change, which drew on scientific advice from many countries, greenhouse gas accumulations in the atmosphere might produce an increase in global mean temperature of between three and eight degrees Fahrenheit in the next century, which could cause a rise in sea levels of up to two feet.

The decision taken by the UN General Assembly in December 1989 to call the Rio conference represented a judgment that the measures of international cooperation launched at Stockholm were not adequate to meet the environmental challenge. Moreover, by defining the Rio meeting as a conference on "environment and development," the Assembly was expressing a new consensus that neither national governments nor international agencies could treat these problems any longer as separate subjects. The alleviation of poverty in poor countries and changes in consumption patterns and production systems in rich countries were now linked inextricably to the environmental agenda.

Huge global conferences like the Rio Earth Summit have at least the positive effect that Samuel Johnson attributed to the prospect of a hanging—they "concentrate the mind wonderfully." In terms of consciousness-raising in governments and in public opinion, Rio was a success. Whether it was a success in terms of dealing with the fundamental problem it was called upon to address—global habitability—it is too early to tell. Our judgment on Rio should be determined by how governments and international agencies follow up its decisions. Although the Agenda 21 action plan covers a wide panorama of issues, we will concentrate here on four that merit priority attention in the months ahead: population, financing, lawmaking, and institutions. Before examining them, however, it will be useful to look briefly at the Rio process and the way governments responded to it.

2

NEW DIPLOMATIC REALITIES

Maurice Strong, the visionary Canadian businessman who served as secretary-general of the Rio meeting—the same position he occupied in Stockholm twenty years earlier—likes to say that "the process is the policy." The process of putting together the Agenda 21 action plan was unusual in two respects. For one thing, it involved an unprecedented mobilization of ideas from the nongovernmental sector. For another, it required achieving consensus among 178 countries.

Representatives of scientific, environmental, religious, business, labor, youth, and women's groups and even of indigenous peoples participated in working groups established to help draft the Agenda 21 chapters. The UNCED Secretariat, drawn by Strong from full-time UN staff and from part-time consultants from many countries, produced a first Agenda 21 draft. The Preparatory Committee for Rio, consisting of all UN members, began serious negotiations on this secretariat document at its fourth and final session in March and April 1992.

This fourth preparatory committee session, or fourth prepcom, served to remind everyone that eco-diplomacy can be even harder than the diplomacy of peace and security. For dealing with problems like Iraq, Cambodia, and Yugoslavia there is a UN Security Council of fifteen members that can make decisions for the entire world community. It is an ideal body for the United States, which like the other permanent members has the right of veto. In the new world of sustainable development negotiations, however, there is no equivalent to the Security Council and no way to create one. Since no purpose would be served by voting on a one-nation one-vote basis—dissenting countries would simply ignore the decisions—the UNCED process sought to work by consensus.

Lowest common denominator diplomacy can be extremely frustrating. In one area after another, Agenda 21 was diluted by veto coalitions of objecting countries. Saudi Arabia, Kuwait, Iran, and other members of OPEC watered down references to energy taxes and renewable energy sources. Malaysia and India resisted international guidelines on national forest management. The Holy See, Argentina, Ireland, and Colombia eliminated the population chapter's references to family planning and contraceptives. The Agenda 21 document that went to Rio from the fourth prepcom had 350 instances of bracketed (disagreed) language, requiring still further compromises at Rio.

Yet the system worked. The final Agenda 21 document, despite the compromises, provides a satisfactory framework for future cooperation. One reason more damage was not done to it was the superb chairmanship of the main committee at Rio by Ambassador Tommy Koh of Singapore, who mobilized peer pressure on governments that sought to press minority positions too far. One of his finest moments came at the committee's concluding session at 4:30 A.M. on June 11, when, to thunderous applause, he made a successful appeal to a Saudi delegate to defer to the wishes of the overwhelming majority on the energy issue.

Rio had been billed by some as the "great shoot-out in the eco-corral"—a North-South confrontation that would rival in intensity the East-West confrontation of the Cold War era. The reality at Rio was a good deal more complicated, revealing a new geometry of international relations. True enough, the Group of 77 (G-77) developing countries (now 129) that had been formed in 1964 continued to function, often putting forward radical demands reminiscent of the "new international economic order" of the 1970s. India and Malaysia proved particularly troublesome, seeking to assign all the blame for poverty and environmental degradation to the developed world, while failing to recognize any need to alter their own self-destructive economic and environmental practices. Many of their statements and proposals revealed a philosophy of one-way sovereignty— the poor countries have the right to share in the wealth and technology of the rich, but should not be asked to undertake any commitments whatsoever with respect to the management of their own affairs. The failure of the NGO community at Rio to refer to this double standard in their daily newspapers and in their parallel NGO forum was one of the signal disappointments of the conference.

Nevertheless, when it came to the crunch, the G-77 were ready to accept reasonable compromises. They did not want to be responsible for the failure of the Earth Summit, which might set back North-South relations for years, not to speak of prospects for both environment and development. The subject matter of Agenda 21 also brought out significant differences among developing countries on issues such as energy, forests, and population. The Latin American countries on the whole provided a moderating element in the G-77, with Brazil as host country performing a skillful role in promoting consensus. Perhaps another factor tempering the demands of the more strident G-77 leaders was the disappearance of the Soviet-led communist bloc that in earlier years had lent them support. The republics of the former Soviet Union and the Central European countries formerly part of the communist world took a low profile at Rio, voicing mainly their new competition with the G-77 for international assistance to clean up the environmental mess left over from communism. As for the European Community and Japan, they went out of their way to demonstrate a new environmental leadership—a positive approach to Agenda 21 and to the Rio conference generally—even if they were not willing to pledge substantial new financial resources in support of Agenda 21 programs.

All this should have provided an excellent setting for the successful exercise of the kind of constructive leadership the United States had demonstrated at the Stockholm conference twenty years earlier. The United States had much going for it at Rio. Despite its failures in energy policy and some recent environmental backsliding by the Bush administration, its overall environment record compared favorably to that of most countries. It was still a major provider of environmental and development aid. It had also pioneered in some of the most important concepts embodied in Agenda 21, such as broad public participation in environmental decision-making through freedom of information, environmental impact statements, and active NGOs. Yet the big story that came out of Rio was "the United States against the world." What had gone wrong?

In the first place, the Bush administration approached the Rio meeting in a deeply divided frame of mind. William Reilly, administrator of the Environmental Protection Agency, and Curtis Bohlen, assistant secretary of state for oceans and international environmental and scientific affairs, saw the Rio meeting as a positive opportunity for American leadership. They shared the basic premises of the conference that a successful partnership in sustainable development would require additional help from developed to developing countries and fundamental changes in rich countries' lifestyles and consumption patterns. They also saw environment and development as reinforcing and not antagonistic concepts, since they believed that adjusting to higher environmental standards could lead to greater productivity and competitiveness. Like the leaders of Japan and the European Community, they were convinced that raising the environmental standards of developing countries could mean a triple benefit for developed countries— the solution of global problems like ozone depletion, greenhouse warming, and biodiversity protection; a more level playing field in international trade for the firms of industrialized countries already subject to strict regulation; and a large and growing market in the developing world for clean technologies and environmental goods and services.

This tendency to see Rio as a foreign policy, economic, and environmental opportunity was not shared elsewhere in the administration—and certainly not in places where support was required. The domestic and economic staff at the White House, joined by Vice President Dan Quayle's Competitiveness Council, viewed Rio as a threat. For them, the Rio agenda meant the loss of jobs and painful economic adjustments in a time of economic difficulty, as well as unwanted pressure to increase foreign aid. It was, moreover, an election year, and in their view there were no votes to be had at Rio. On the contrary, Ross Perot's presidential challenge seemed to make it more urgent than ever to hold on to conservative Republican voters who would be hostile to the concessions the United States would be asked to make. Elsewhere in the administration—in the Interior, Commerce, and Treasury departments—Rio was regarded with suspicion, at best with indifference.

For a secretary of state or a national security advisor seeking to give content to a president's "new world order," Rio might have seemed a perfect opportunity. Yet neither James Baker nor Brent Scowcroft, preoccupied as they were with events in the disintegrating communist world and in the Middle East after

Desert Storm, seemed very much interested. Perhaps they were also reluctant to assume the political burden of taking on the conservatives in the Republican party for whom Rio was anathema. In any event, without strong leadership from the top level of state or NSC it was impossible to develop affirmative U.S. policies for the Earth Summit. The interagency process, left to spin its wheels at a low level, produced little agreement, except perhaps on what the United States would *not* agree to at the conference.

An administration in such a mood of negativism and organizational disarray provided fertile ground for any disaster waiting to happen, and one soon came in the unexpected form of the Biodiversity Convention. No one at a senior level had given much thought to this treaty, which was intended to protect the diversity of genetic resources, species, and habitats of plants and animals threatened with extinction. High-level attention had focused on the Global Warming Treaty, and it was all the State Department and EPA could do to persuade the White House to agree to it, even with timetables and targets removed. The U.S. government had little interest in completing the biodiversity negotiations in time for signature at Rio, and neither for that matter, did Maurice Strong, who saw that the inclusion in that treaty of biotechnology issues could be a source of controversy.

The biodiversity negotiations took place in Nairobi under the auspices of UNEP, whose director, Mustafa Tolba, saw the speedy completion of the treaty in time for Rio as a means of restoring some of the leadership role in environmental matters that he had lost when the climate change negotiations were entrusted to a body separate from UNEP established by the General Assembly. To make matters worse, the Kuala Lumpur Conference of developing countries hosted by Malaysia in April encouraged some in the G-77 to see the Biodiversity Convention as an opportunity to make extreme demands on the issues of technology transfer and financial control. The unfortunate U.S. delegation, headed by an office director in Curtis Bohlen's bureau, found itself in an impossible situation. It had no support from senior political levels of the government, and no high level representations were made to turn around the situation in foreign capitals. A few days before the Rio conference began, the administration announced that it would not sign the Biodiversity Convention because it was "seriously flawed."

Seriously flawed it certainly was. As will shortly be explained, the convention failed to provide adequate protection to intellectual property rights and gave an unacceptable degree of financial control to developing countries. Yet a whole week was to pass in Rio before the American delegation explained the reasons for its opposition, or even had a copy of the convention to give to the press. During this time the biodiversity issue dominated media and NGO discussions, and the U.S. position was interpreted as hostility not only to biodiversity protection but to the whole Rio agenda. A half-hearted effort was made to preserve some unity with its industrialized allies, many of whom shared the American objections, but it quickly fell apart, as political pressures to sign at Rio mounted from the allies' NGOs as well as from developing countries. Some allies seemed even to make a point of distancing themselves on this issue from an unpopular United States. White House officials, now in an increasingly defensive and embittered mood, began to issue statements criticizing both U.S. allies and developing countries, denouncing environmental "extremists" and describing the Earth Summit itself as a "circus." When Reilly tried to save the situation through a message to the White House proposing modest changes in the convention, his memorandum was leaked to the press, thus humiliating the leader of the U.S. delegation and deepening the country's isolation.

Shortly after the conference, Reilly offered with remarkable candor some reasons of his own for the American failure at Rio:

> We assigned a low priority to the negotiation of the biodiversity treaty, were slow to engage the climate issue, were last to commit our President to attend Rio. We put our delegation together late, and we committed few resources. No doubt, this contributed to negative feelings toward the United States.
>
> For me personally, it was like a bungee jump. You dive into space secured by a line on your leg and trust it pulls you up before you smash into the ground. It doesn't typically occur to you that someone might cut your line.[1]

Paradoxically, despite this fiasco, the Agenda 21 negotiations were concluded successfully, and the U.S. delegation under Reilly and Bohlen made positive contributions to the outcome within the limit of their instructions. The question now is how the diplomatic achievements of Rio can be translated into action, and how the United States can improve its eco-diplomacy in the future.

3
POPULATION

Without greatly expanded efforts to slow and eventually stabilize the rapid rates of population growth in the developing world, no action plan for sustainable development will be worth the paper it is written on. The Rio meeting was widely criticized in the press for neglecting the population problem or treating it with excessive caution. A comment in *Time*'s cover story was typical: "Unfortunately, the summit's capitulation on the population question will probably nullify whatever progress the conference makes on other issues."[1] That judgment was clearly wrong. This is not to say, however, that population was treated in the UNCED process with the priority and sense of urgency that it deserved.

The true story of population at UNCED is complicated and requires careful analysis of the evolution of the Agenda 21 program of action, which dedicated a ten-page chapter to "Demographic Dynamics and Sustainability." The draft of this chapter that was presented to the fourth prepcom in New York called for "universal access to family planning services and the provision of safe contraceptives." The Holy See launched a major diplomatic effort to eliminate this language, probably the strongest lobbying campaign it had ever undertaken in the UN, reflecting the strong views held by Pope John Paul II.

Argentina, Colombia, Ireland, and other countries with large Catholic populations supported the Holy See's campaign. The American delegation, reflecting the Bush administration's alliance with the right to life movement, sought a compromise that would recognize the Holy See's objections to the phrases "family planning" and "contraception" while preserving the essential elements of established UN population policy.

As a result, the population chapter in Agenda 21 that was passed to Rio from the fourth prepcom contained the following new language:

> Governments should take active steps to implement, as a matter of urgency . . . measures to ensure that women and men have the same right to decide freely and responsibly on the number and spacing of their children, to have access to the information, education and means, as appropriate, to enable them to exercise this right in keeping with their freedom, dignity and personally held values taking into account ethical and cultural considerations."

This more diplomatic rewrite of the original language to which the Holy See objected was supplemented by a recommendation that governments should make available to their populations "affordable, accessible services" for "the responsible planning of family size."*

---

* The appendix to this essay contains relevant excerpts from Agenda 21 on population, financing, and institutions, as well as some key articles from the Conventions on Biodiversity and Climate Change.

Nafis Sadik, the able Pakistani woman who heads the UN Population Fund, clearly spoke for the overwhelming majority of delegations when she addressed the Rio Plenary and stated that this language in the population chapter embodied the UN consensus established at the Mexico City conference in 1984 and repeated in subsequent UN pronouncements that "information, education and means" should include "all medically approved and appropriate means of family planning." In other words, the use of medically accepted contraceptives was sanctioned by the agreed language, even if the word contraceptives was not used, as indeed it has never been used in any UN pronouncement on the subject. While the original language was clearly preferable for family planning advocates, it is hard to see how its replacement by the new language will make much practical difference in the real world.

The population chapter of Agenda 21 approved at Rio, moreover, contained other helpful recommendations for the future. Countries are urged, for example, to assess their "national population carrying capacity" and to establish "national population goals and programs that are consistent with their national environment and development plans for sustainability." Perhaps most important of all, the chapter on population closes by citing the secretariat estimate that implementing these and other recommendations on population will require an increase in the total amount of resources devoted to population activities in developing countries from $4.5 billion per year to an average of $7 billion a year in the period

1992 to 2000, half of which will be required from international assistance. Though not explicitly stated, this estimate is consistent with reaching the UN Population Fund's goal for the year 2000 of $9 billion in annual spending for population activities, double the present level.

The fact that a compromise had been reached on population in the fourth prepcom meant that there was no need to reopen the subject at the Agenda 21 negotiations in Rio. But this did not mean that population was off the agenda, as many inattentive observers concluded. The population chapter in Agenda 21, was, after all, part of the action plan formally approved at Rio. Furthermore, a large number of delegates, including delegates from developing countries, noted the necessity of action on the population front in their general debate statements. Maurice Strong himself at the very outset of the general debate warned that population trends were unsustainable and that measures should be taken to stabilize world population as soon as possible.

The key question about population at the Rio meeting, therefore, is not whether the compromise text provides an adequate framework for future action. It does. Rather, the key question is whether the governments of developed and developing countries will now demonstrate the political will and commit the necessary resources to deal with the world population crisis before it is too late.

If this statement seems too apocalyptic, consider the latest UN projections of future population growth which have been raised in the light of recent developments. According to its medium or most likely projection (which assumes a continued slow decline in fertility levels), world population, which was 1.5 billion in 1900 and which has reached 5.5 billion today, will reach 8.5 billion by 2025 and 10 billion by 2050 and will not stabilize until it reaches 11.6 billion in 2150.

The UN's low or most optimistic projection, which assumes (unrealistically) that the world could reach replacement rate fertility (an average of slightly more than two children per couple) by the period 2010 to 2015, is for population stabilization at 7.8 billion by the middle of the next century. The UN's high or most pessimistic projection is for a world population of 12.5 billion in 2050 heading toward 28 billion a century later. Where in the range of 7.8 to 28 billion population does finally stabilize will fundamentally determine the prospects of the human race not only for a habitable planet but for human rights, political stability, and world peace.

Global population numbers, frightening as they are, tell only part of the story. It is necessary to look at the numbers for key developing countries. Again according to the latest UN medium projection for 2025, Nigeria will grow from 108 million to 281 million, Egypt from 52 to 90 million, Ethiopia from 49 to 126 million, Iraq from 19 to 50 million, Iran from 55 to 114 million, Bangladesh from 115 to 235 million, India from 853 to 1,442 million, China from 1,139 to 1,512 million, Brazil from 150 to 246 million, and Mexico from 88 to 150 million.

No government, no academic expert, has the faintest idea of how to provide adequate food, housing, health care, education, and gainful employment to such exploding numbers of people, particularly as they crowd into megacities like Mexico City, Cairo, and Calcutta. The growing numbers of desperate poor implied in these figures will only accelerate the ferocious assault on the world's environment now underway in Africa, Asia, and Latin America. Can anyone doubt that if even these medium growth figures are realized, our children and grandchildren will witness unprecedented misery, worldwide violence, and a tidal wave of unwanted immigration coming their way?

Despite gradual declines in fertility, the growing number of couples in the child-bearing years in developing countries adds a huge built-in momentum to present rates of population growth and a special urgency to action in the next decade. As Robert McNamara recently pointed out, for example, if Pakistan continues on its present course with very gradual reduction in fertility, its population of 115 million will rise to 556 million. If, however, it were to introduce during this decade a very effective family planning program, which it does not now have, it could hold its eventual population to 334 million. The 222 million difference is nearly double Pakistan's present population.

The UN has scheduled an International Conference on Population and Development for 1994 in Cairo. If Rio's sustainable development goals are to be met, countries will have to take this population conference much more seriously at the highest levels of government than they took previous UN population meetings. For developing countries, the 1994 meeting should be the occasion to set target figures at which their populations should be stabilized and target dates by which replacement rate fertility will be realized in order to reach those population targets. In carrying out these policies, developing countries will need to focus not just on the provision of family planning services but on education, maternal and child health care, and women's rights. They should also respect the freedom of individual choice and the respect for diversity of ethical and cultural values called for in Agenda 21's population chapter.

To do all this will require large increases in the budgets of developing countries for population activities and related social spending, as well as courageous political leadership. One measure of how far they have to go is that only about 30 to 40 percent of couples in the developing world outside of China are presently using contraceptives. There are about 300 million couples in these countries who lack access to modern means of family planning. UN surveys suggest that 125 million of these couples would use contraceptives now if they were made available—and that this number would grow rapidly with education, health services, and the realization of women's rights.

For the developed countries, the challenge ahead is no less formidable. It will take a large increase in international aid for family planning if the $9 billion a year called for by the UN Population Fund is to be found for family planning and related population activities in developing countries by the year 2000. If, as the Population Fund estimates, at least one-half of this sum is needed from international sources—and if the United States were to provide 20 percent of that total—it would mean a U.S. population budget by the year 2000 of about $900 million annually. U.S. funding of population assistance is now stuck at a plateau of $250 million a year and declining in real terms.

In 1985, Ronald Reagan, deferring to the right to life movement, cut off all U.S. aid to the International Planned Parenthood Federation (IPPF) and the UN Population Fund. The cutoff has been continued by President Bush, notwithstanding strenuous efforts by the Congress to reverse it. Until this policy is changed the United States will be unable to resume its previous leadership role in multilateral population efforts.

The justification given for the present policy is that IPPF gives abortion counseling and that the Population Fund has a program in China whose one child policy is seen as having unacceptable coercive elements. The statement about IPPF is true, but irrelevant: by blocking family planning aid to IPPF the present policy is only adding to the number of abortions in developing countries, putting at risk the lives of tens of thousands of women without access to medical care.

The statement about the Population Fund is also irrelevant, since its programs in China support contraceptive production and the development of population information and do not fund operational activities that could be considered coercive. In any event, the administration could demonstrate its reservations about alleged abuses in China's population programs by accepting the compromise proposed years ago by the U.S. Congress and acceptable to the Population Fund: the United States can earmark its contributions for countries other than China, and the Population Fund will freeze the size of the China program at current levels.

A generation ago a U.S. Ambassador to the United Nations described world population trends as "a prescription for tragedy and chaos." U.S. interests, he added, demand that UN Population Fund "should grow rapidly . . . to a point where it will be making an important impact on world population."[2] The ambassador in question was George Bush. His judgments are as valid today as they were then. To provide U.S. leadership in meeting the population challenge to global habitability will be more difficult now. It will also be more critical.

4

FINANCING

One of the fundamental requirements for the
successful implementation of Rio's Agenda 21
action plan will be a successful answer to the
question: Where is the money coming from?
The premise of the Rio meeting was that if
developing countries are to carry out their
obligations under Agenda 21, they must be
helped to find a sufficient amount of external
resources. These resources could be made
available in a variety of ways—from greater
access to markets, improved terms of trade,
debt relief, private investment, technical aid,
or official development assistance (ODA).

Although all of these subjects were touched
on in the Rio debates and in the Agenda 21
action plan, the central focus was on the
volume of ODA and on the institutions and
procedures through which it would be made
available. That controversy was resolved at Rio
only in part.

The General Assembly resolution laying
out the mandate for the Earth Summit called
for "new and additional" financial resources to
be made available from developed to developing countries. Nearly all countries, including
Japan and the members of the European Community, accepted that "new and additional"
meant, among other things, new and additional ODA.

The U.S. delegation, however, was under strict instructions to make no commitment of this kind. New and additional resources for sustainable development, in the U.S. view, could come from private investment, but any increased ODA for this purpose would have to come from a reduction of ODA for other purposes—in other words, from reprogramming within a fixed ODA ceiling.

The intransigence of the United States on ODA was matched by the demagogy of the "North-South cold warriors" in the G-77. India, Malaysia, and others pressed for a new "Green Fund," separate from existing international financial institutions, for the provision of resources "without any conditionality" and for management according to "democratic" principles—meaning one-nation one-vote and an automatic G-77 majority. In the preparations for Rio, this was the official G-77 position, supported vigorously by China. But it became clear by the fourth prepcom that the G-77 would abandon these unrealistic demands if the United States and the developed countries would come forward with significant commitments to new and additional ODA.

The North-South division on financing assumed particular importance when Maurice Strong responded to the request in the General Assembly's original UNCED resolution that his secretariat "quantify the financial requirements" for the successful implementation of UNCED decisions and identify possible sources of additional funding. When this was done for each chapter in Agenda 21 the final numbers seemed awesome: The average annual costs in the period 1993 to 2000 for implementing the action plan in developing countries was $600 billion. Of this amount about $475 billion, some 80 percent, would have to come from the developing countries' own resources; some $125 billion, or about 20 percent, would be needed from donor countries in the form of ODA. Since the annual volume of ODA was now only $55 billion, this would mean a $70 billion increase in ODA above current levels. Donor countries refused to ratify these secretariat figures, and succeeded in including language in the Agenda 21 financing section at Rio specifying that they were "indicative and order of magnitude estimates only, and have not been reviewed by governments."

Developing countries were quick to point out that the figure of $125 billion of ODA, large as it seemed, could be nearly achieved if the developed countries would raise the level of their ODA as a fraction of GNP from the present average of about 0.35 percent to the target of 0.7 percent approved some years earlier (over U.S. opposition) by the General Assembly. The G-77 sought at Rio to commit the developed countries to reach the 0.7 percent target by the year 2000. The Nordic countries were prepared to accept this demand, while most other donors were prepared to reaffirm the 0.7 percent target as a goal to be reached "as soon as possible." The United States, whose level of ODA has slipped in recent years to 0.15 percent of GNP, was one of several donors whose only agreement was to make their "best efforts" to increase their ODA.

Even the hardest-line G-77 members did not expect commitments at Rio to an immediate $70 billion increase in annual ODA. Indeed, the developing countries accepted the unreality of such numbers at a time of global recession, when special demands were being made on Western donors to assist the republics of the former Soviet Union and the countries of East Central Europe. They accepted, too, that it would be years before additional ODA flows in that amount could find their counterpart in sound development and environment projects. Most of the G-77 probably agreed with Maurice Strong's estimates that initial commitments by donor countries at Rio to additional ODA in the amount of $5–$10 billion a year would be sufficient to secure their agreement to the Agenda 21 program.

But what came from the European Community countries and Japan at Rio by way of new ODA was ambiguous and hard to quantify; it certainly fell short of that sum. The only pledge from the United States, $150 million in additional bilateral forest assistance, was far from meeting the minimum requirements of even the more moderate developing nations. It looked at one point as if the Rio meeting would come apart on this question.

The *deus ex machina* who averted this Greek tragedy in the making was an unexpected player in the Rio drama—none other than Lewis Preston, the new president of the World Bank Group. In what was arguably the decisive address at the Earth summit, Preston said the World Bank Group would be supporting developing countries in designing environmental action plans to carry out the UNCED agenda. His institutions, he promised, would expand their activity in areas such as water supply and sanitation, agricultural research and extension, energy conservation, reforestation, family planning, health, and education.

Then came Preston's crucial announcement: He would propose an "earth increment" for the tenth replenishment of the International Development Association (IDA-10) covering the period 1993 to 1995, an amount additional to the volume of resources needed to maintain the funding level for the ninth IDA (IDA-9) replenishment in real terms. Since IDA-9 was funded at $15.5 billion, this meant Preston would be seeking an earth increment on top of a floor of about $18 billion for the three-year period. In addition, he said he would propose an annual allocation of the World Bank's net income as the World Bank's own contribution to augment whatever earth increment might be forthcoming from donor country contributions.

Preston's statement provided the essential minimum of prospective funding that enabled the G-77 to abandon its "Green Fund" demand and close on an agreed Agenda 21 financing text. The formula was deceptively simple— "special consideration should be given" to Preston's statement as a way of helping "the poorest countries meet their sustainable development objectives as contained in Agenda 21."

Resolving the ODA stalemate at Rio, however, was one thing; persuading donor countries to follow through with an IDA-10 replenishment large enough to secure developing country cooperation on Agenda 21 may be considerably more difficult in the economic and political environment that lies immediately ahead. A good faith implementation of Preston's proposal would imply a minimum target for IDA-10 of $22.5 billion over the 1993 to 1995 period—$18 billion to maintain the IDA-9 funding in real terms, $3 billion in additional contributions from donor governments, and $1.5 billion from World Bank earnings.

The U.S. share of the additional $1 billion in annual contributions over the real value of IDA-9 required of governments would be $200 million. The willingness of the administration and Congress to deliver on this relatively small earth increment will be another test of the U.S. commitment to play its full part in making a success of the "partnership in sustainable development" that the Rio meeting was intended to launch.

Donor countries, of course, will need to make fundamental decisions in the months ahead not only on the IDA-10 replenishment but on possible earth increments in the regional development banks for Asia, Africa, and Latin America and in bilateral aid programs. They will also need to consider increased funding for the UN Development Program (UNDP), which will be the principal vehicle for training people and strengthening environmental institutions in developing countries.

Equally important, donors will need to look harder at how environmental and developmental considerations can be balanced and reconciled in aid programs. Large hydroelectric projects in countries such as China and India are likely to pose difficult choices with sensitive political dimensions for multilateral and bilateral aid agencies, as environmental NGOs seek to block such projects while developing countries object to the imposition of new external constraints on their "right to development."

Clearly what is needed now is not just additional funding but an improved policy dialogue between donors and recipients. To this end, individual developing countries should meet under the auspices of World Bank consultative groups and UNDP roundtables to negotiate long-term compacts with bilateral and multilateral aid donors on the funding and execution of the country's projects in the framework of Agenda 21 programs.

This policy dialogue will only serve its purpose if it helps to unblock the internal obstacles that still impede sustainable development in most developing countries. A recent UNDP Human Development Report estimated that developing countries themselves could release as much as $50 billion a year for meeting their sustainable development objectives if they lowered their military expenditures, privatized public enterprises, corrected distorted development priorities, rooted out corruption, and generally improved national governance.

As the international community looks at the financial followup to Rio, it will be taking a particularly careful look at the Global Environment Facility (GEF), the three-year pilot program of $1.3 billion established in November 1990 and operated by the World Bank, UNEP, and UNDP. The World Bank serves as administrator and repository of the facility and is responsible for major investments, while UNEP provides the scientific expertise and UNDP handles technical assistance for investment studies and small grants to grassroots organizations.

The basic mission of the GEF is to cover the agreed incremental costs that developing countries incur in order to achieve agreed global benefits, including their obligations under certain global environmental conventions. It presently funds projects in four areas of global environmental concern—climate change, biodiversity conservation, international waters (oceans and international river systems), and protection of the ozone layer.

Developing countries called for a number of changes in the GEF both in the pre-Rio negotiations and at Rio itself. These are now being dealt with in the GEF restructuring that was launched by its participants at a meeting last April. One important change under consideration is the enlargement of subjects eligible for GEF funding to include land degradation issues, primarily desertification and deforestation, when they can be related to the four focal areas of GEF concern. Another likely change would be to permit universal membership in the GEF and thus participation in its governance by recipients as well as donor countries. A third change, consequent on the second, is the possible establishment of a "double majority voting mechanism." Where decisions of the GEF participants cannot be made by consensus, which is the normal procedure, they will have to be adopted with the approval both of a majority of the participants on a one-nation one-vote basis and of a second majority representing a majority of the financial contributions.

Completion of the GEF restructuring exercise in a way that satisfies developed and developing countries is essential if the GEF is to fulfill its original purpose as the principal vehicle for funding environmental projects and programs of global concern and as the financing mechanism for the funds established under the biodiversity, global warming, and other special environmental conventions still to come, such as those on forests and desertification. It will also be necessary if the donors are to increase their contributions for the 1994–1996 triennium beyond the GEF's pilot stage, as some donors have proposed, to magnitudes such as $3 or $4 billion. This will be yet another test of whether Rio's global partnership concept has real meaning when it comes to the critical question of money.

In this new era of eco-diplomacy, the leaders of developing countries have demonstrated that the developed countries' concern over how they use their forests and design their energy strategies provides them with new leverage to seek increases in ODA and other forms of international assistance. At the same time, the leaders of developed countries have been given new arguments with which to appeal to their parliaments and peoples on behalf of increases in ODA, since such earth increments can be viewed as necessary investments in the protection of a shared global environment of which the domestic environment is an interdependent part. It remains to be seen whether these new political realities will provide the new and additional resources that developing countries need to carry out their obligations under the action plan of Agenda 21.

5

LAWMAKING

The twenty years between the Stockholm and Rio conferences have seen a veritable explosion in international environmental lawmaking. The international community is not ready for some kind of world environmental authority with the power to make laws for member countries, much less to enforce such laws with an international police force. Instead, we are seeing treaty-making of the classical kind, involving mutual restraints and reciprocal concessions entered into voluntarily on the basis of reciprocal advantage.

Yet there are a number of ways in which international treaty-making on subjects like ozone, global warming, and biodiversity is different from treaty-making on nonenvironmental concerns. One is the necessity of securing the participation of major developing countries who might be considered marginal on many nonenvironmental subjects. If China and India go forward with their plans to triple the burning of coal as their principal source of energy in the next generation, for example, their contribution to global warming will more than offset the greenhouse gas reductions that developed countries are likely to achieve. From this there follow two other differences of eco-lawmaking: first, to secure the participation of developing countries it is necessary to have a treaty regime that gives them the financial and technical means to perform their environmental obligations; second, their obligations must be defined in less stringent terms, at least for an initial period. These new eco-treaties also require a built-in process of adjustment so that commitments can be altered in the light of new scientific evidence. The Montreal Protocol on Substances that Deplete the Ozone Layer is a recent example of how this can be done. The new international environmental law, in this sense, comes to us on the installment plan.

A formidable agenda of international and domestic environmental lawmaking lies before governments in the post-Rio years. One of the Earth Summit's accomplishments was the approval of the Rio Declaration on Environment and Development, with its twenty-seven principles as guides to government policy. The declaration contains what lawyers call "soft law"—less than compulsory guidelines for government behavior. Some of these principles— such as the obligation of states to notify and consult with other potentially affected states on activities that may have a significant transboundary effect—will hopefully be embodied one day in international treaty law and usher in a new system for settling environmental disputes. Other principles—such as those calling for environmental impact assessments and compensation to victims of pollution—can influence lawmaking at the national level.

Another product of Rio—the nonlegally binding statement of principles on the sustainable development of forests—was a disappointment to many countries and NGOs. It does little more than exhort countries in general terms to manage their forests in a sustainable way in return for international help. Rio left the way open, however, for the future negotiation of a binding forest convention. Given the strong opposition to such a treaty by Malaysia, India, and some other tropical forest countries, the choice now lies between doing nothing and negotiating a less-than-universal treaty with those countries such as Brazil that are willing to take conservation commitments if they are given the means to carry them out. The success of such a limited treaty regime might eventually persuade the forest holdouts to change their minds, especially as they perceive the growing danger of boycotts of their tropical timber exports by NGOs in Western countries.

Rio also produced a decision, strongly supported by African countries, to negotiate a convention on desertification. This subject may lend itself more easily to the negotiation of regional treaty regimes for different continents than a global convention. The G-77, however, may feel its bargaining power can only be preserved by opting for a universal approach.

Trade and environment was one of Rio's most controversial items, undoubtedly stimulated by the U.S. ban on tuna caught by Mexican fishermen without sufficient measures for the protection of dolphins. The rules of the General Agreement on Tariffs and Trade (GATT) as interpreted by its tuna/dolphin panel do not permit the unilateral imposition of trade restrictions as a means of defense against an environmentally harmful production process where the restricted product does not itself pose environmental harm. A new GATT negotiation on this subject will be needed to try to reconcile trade and environmental objectives. The threat of additional trade restrictions for environmental purposes may also provide a stimulus for the negotiation of minimum environmental standards in particular industrial and agricultural sectors.

There is also unfinished business ahead with respect to the two conventions signed at the Rio meeting. The Framework Convention on Climate Change is the first international legal instrument to recognize that global warming is a threat to the planet. Its parties are committed to the goal of stabilizing greenhouse gas concentrations in the atmosphere at a level that would prevent dangerous interference with the earth's climate, and to do so in a time frame that will permit ecosystems to adapt.

All countries, both developed and developing, are committed under the convention to formulate, implement, publish, and regularly update national programs containing measures to mitigate climate change by limiting human-generated greenhouse gas emissions and by enhancing forest "sinks" for these gasses, thus subjecting themselves to regular review and peer pressure. In addition, the developed countries accept the aim of returning individually or jointly to their 1990 levels of carbon dioxide and other greenhouse gas emissions at an unspecified time in the future. The developed countries are also pledged to provide new and additional financial resources to help developing countries cover costs of carrying out their commitments under the convention.

The U.S. government has been roundly criticized at home and abroad for blocking the inclusion of a firm commitment to reduce carbon dioxide emissions to 1990 levels by the year 2000, a commitment Japan and the European Community were willing to undertake. Even without that commitment, however, the treaty is an important step forward. Nevertheless, a future U.S. administration may wish to reconsider the possibility of accepting targets and timetables for the reduction of carbon dioxide emissions when the parties of the treaty review its adequacy, as they are required to do, within one year of its coming into force and periodically thereafter. At some point in this decade, new scientific evidence may provide a new sense of urgency to support these targets. Moreover, as many experts maintain, the measures which the United States is already undertaking at the federal and state levels—such as tougher energy efficiency standards for appliances and equipment, government encouragement to alternative fuel vehicles, and incentives to electrical utilities to improve efficiency—may make it possible for the country to stay within the 1990 levels of carbon dioxide and other greenhouse gas emissions by the year 2000 without much difficulty. Of course, a substantial tax on gasoline, coupled with some kind of carbon tax on the use of coal and other fossil fuels, would have the triple advantage of assuring American leadership in international cooperation on global warming while also raising substantial revenue and reducing U.S. dependence on foreign oil.

U.S. leadership can play an important role in assuring a prompt start of the Climate Change Treaty. In his speech at Rio, President Bush promised to seek its speedy approval in the Senate, to help fund developing countries' efforts to compile inventories of their greenhouse gas emissions, and to maintain a high level of scientific research on global warming—with $1.4 billion proposed for the current fiscal year. He also promised to submit a U.S. action plan to reduce greenhouse gas emissions for scrutiny by the rest of the world at an international conference that he proposed be held in 1993. If the United States follows through on these promises—and if other countries cooperate on this prompt start agenda—the Climate Convention will have a good chance of fulfilling the hopes of those who labored so long and hard in its completion.

One final piece of unfinished lawmaking that must be mentioned is the adjustment of the objectionable provisions of the Convention on Biological Diversity so that the United States can become a party. As argued earlier, the Bush administration should be faulted not for refusing to sign the convention, but for the mishandling of its negotiation. The provisions on technology transfer and financing are seriously flawed, as the administration has maintained. Article 16, entitled "Access to and Transfer of Technology," is a five-paragraph hodgepodge of contradictory language with a strong political bias against the protection of intellectual property rights. One of its controlling provisions commits the parties to cooperate "in order to ensure that such rights are supportive of and do not run counter to" the objectives of the convention, which include technology-sharing with developing countries.

The ambiguities and contradictions in Article 16 fail to assure adequate protection of intellectual property rights which are essential for the U.S. biotechnology, pharmaceutical and agribusiness industries—industries where this country still has a competitive advantage. The article would also create an undesirable precedent for trade negotiations on the same issues that are still underway in the Uruguay Round and in bilateral negotiations. The developing countries have a valid claim to benefit financially from their genetic resources found and exploited by biotech and other companies of the industrialized world and to have access to the technology developed through the use of these resources. That aim, however, should be accomplished by agreements freely made between developing countries and private firms. Moreover, access to technology can be purchased with the help of financial resources provided by bilateral or multilateral aid programs; it should not be subject to forcible appropriation by governments.

Article 21 of the convention, entitled "Financial Mechanism," is even more objectionable. Instead of using the formula of the Climate Change Convention, which as an interim measure provided for voluntary contributions to be administered by the GEF, this article suggests that the parties to the convention will decide by a one-nation one-vote majority system what amount of money will be assessed against the donors and will also decide on this basis on the program priorities and eligibility criteria for access to these resources. Even if a U.S. administration were to sign such a treaty, it is hard to imagine that a two-thirds majority would be available in the Senate to advise and consent to its ratification.

A solution to this difficulty, however, may be available with a little help from the United Kingdom, Germany, Japan, and other industrialized countries that share our concerns on one or both of these articles and would like to see the United States as a party. Although these countries have signed the treaty, they could withhold ratification pending negotiation of a treaty protocol that would redefine the terms of the two articles in ways that are generally acceptable. This could provide negotiating leverage with the G-77, who will not wish to have a treaty without key European nations and Japan.

The changes the United States seeks, after all, are modest and reasonable: first, elimination of the provision that intellectual property rights are to be subordinated to the purpose of the convention; second, incorporation of the GEF formula on financing that was acceptable to the G-77 in the Climate Convention. If, as seems likely, the GEF can be restructured to the mutual satisfaction of both developed and developing countries, the negotiation of a protocol to the Convention on Biological Diversity will be greatly facilitated.

6

INSTITUTIONS

There was universal agreement at Rio that the success of the Earth Summit would ultimately be determined not by what was said there but by what countries and international agencies actually did afterward. The world has witnessed too many conferences that merely produced statements of good intentions. A critical question throughout the UNCED process was what kind of new or improved international institutions should be created to assure the implementation of the Agenda 21 program. Considering that Agenda 21, as noted earlier, covers over 400 pages of text with forty chapters and 115 program areas, it is not such an easy question to answer.

Yet a consensus on institutions evolved during the Rio preparatory process and was confirmed at Rio with remarkably little controversy. A new high level Commission on Sustainable Development is to be created under the Economic and Social Council (ECOSOC) "to examine the progress of the implementation of Agenda 21 at the national, regional and international levels." Details on the membership of the commission, on the frequency, duration, and venue of its meetings, and on its relationship to other UN bodies dealing with environment and development are to be decided by the 47th General Assembly, on the basis of recommendations from the UN secretary-general, assisted by the secretary-general of UNCED.

The principal task of the new commission will be to monitor the implementation of Agenda 21 by governments and UN agencies. The Rio institutional proposals break new ground in calling for the close association, with the work of the commission, of multilateral financial institutions, NGOs, and the business community. They also call for consideration to be given to the creation of a "high-level advisory board" consisting of eminent persons knowledgeable about environment and development and appointed in their personal capacity. In all these ways the intention is to replicate the outreach to groups and individuals outside the UN system that characterized the Rio preparatory process. There is even a reference in the Rio institutional decision to the possible establishment of a non-governmental Earth Council, to be a kind of environmental conscience watching the behavior of governments.

Rio also proposed that the secretary-general of the UN should establish a highly qualified secretariat within the UN Secretariat to support the commission, drawing on some of the persons involved in the Rio preparations. The secretary-general is also asked to organize a new mechanism to coordinate the activities of the entire UN system, including all the specialized agencies and operating programs, in pursuit of sustainable development goals. UNDP and UNEP are to be strengthened as part of the new sustainable development structure.

The institutional innovations emerging from Rio are timely because they come in the midst of efforts by UN members to restructure and strengthen ECOSOC and of efforts by the new secretary-general to streamline the UN Secretariat. The new concept of sustainable development, designed to marry environment and development into a coherent whole, could be the basis of a reorientation of the whole UN system for greater effectiveness. But there is no way this will happen unless governments devote more high-level attention to the UN's economic work than they have in the past.

Hard decisions lie ahead on institutional questions. What kind of persons should governments send as their principal representatives to the Sustainable Development Commission—Cabinet level officers or senior career officials? Should these persons be from ministries of foreign affairs, finance, overseas development, or environment? If the Sustainable Development Commission performs all the functions foreseen for it, what is left for a restructured ECOSOC to do in its newly-agreed policy and coordination segments? How can the commission encourage governments to support the coordination process by insisting, as they have failed to do in the past, that their officials speak with one voice in different UN bodies? How can the international financial institutions, where the big money is, be persuaded to cooperate with a subsidiary body of an ECOSOC whose track record is less than inspiring? And how can traditional UN procedures be revised to assure that the broad and fruitful NGO participation that characterized the Rio process will be continued?

There are other hard questions as well. Should the new secretariat serving the Sustainable Development Commission be part of the huge UN Department of Economic and Social Development (DESD)? If it is, should DESD relinquish its technical assistance functions to UNDP, so that it can achieve greater credibility in its coordination of the sustainable development activities of UN programs and specialized agencies? If it is to be separate from DESD, what will be the division of responsibilities between the two, since just about everything the DESD does relates to sustainable development? And what precisely will be the division of functions between the new commission and its secretariat support staff, on the one hand, and the UNEP Governing Council and Secretariat in Nairobi, on the other? To be sure, UNEP has a clear continuing role with its Earthwatch program of scientific monitoring, with organizing cooperation on the cleanup of the Mediterranean and other regional seas, with promoting environmentally sound technologies, and with furthering the development of environmental law. But what becomes of UNEP's role in "policy guidance and coordination in the field of the environment"—a mandate reconfirmed in the agreed Rio institutional chapter? How does that get reconciled with the role of the new commission? And, finally, how can the Sustainable Development Commission and its secretariat promote cooperation with the wide variety of regional organizations like the European Community which deal with environment and development issues outside the United Nations?

Governments will need to think hard about these and other questions if all-too-familiar UN turf battles and duplication are to be avoided. They will also need to develop common positions in a powerful coalition of developed and developing countries if they are to shape the embryonic institutions for sustainable development in ways that strengthen UN effectiveness and serve their common national interests.

7

CONCLUSION

The road from Rio, it would seem, will be a difficult one, particularly for the United States. We will need to come up with a new population policy, additional flows of ODA, a greater commitment to environmental lawmaking, and more coherent leadership in the United Nations.

How can this be reconciled with the power of the right to life movement, a weak domestic economy, and the understandable desire of Americans to devote more resources to neglected domestic problems? Clearly, for the next president, restoring American leadership on the post-Rio agenda will be a challenge.

Two things that must be done are obvious. First, the president must define a new post–cold war foreign policy for the American people in convincing terms. As is argued in the recent report of the Carnegie Endowment National Commission on America and the New World, of which this writer was a member, there are now four overriding national concerns of the American people in events beyond our borders: promoting democratic values and institutions, maintaining an open and growing world economy, building a new system of collective security, and assuring global habitability.[1] Our success or failure on these four foreign policy goals will have a profound impact on our domestic welfare. Moreover, achieving these goals will require more money. This is particularly true for global habitability. As that very practical banker, Lewis Preston, said at Rio: "The question is not whether we can afford to do it, the question is, can we afford *not* to do it." Unless we can deal responsibly with the U.S. deficit and fundamentally alter our current spending priorities, there is no way we can respond adequately to the post-Rio agenda.

The second obvious thing to be done is to reshape our governmental institutions to enable them to cope with this revised set of critical foreign policy objectives. Issues of global habitability can no longer be regarded as marginal, "soft" subjects, not worthy of the continuing attention of the secretary of state and national security advisor. We need improved mechanisms to assure a unified approach by our cabinet departments to sustainable development issues. Perhaps the time has come to rewrite the National Security Act of 1947 to redefine national security in terms of the four objectives laid out by the Carnegie Commission. Such a statutory revision might help to assure that our central coordinating mechanism for foreign policy was properly staffed to meet the new global challenges.

It is not enough for a president to make an occasional speech saying there is no longer a clear division between domestic and foreign affairs. He must act as if he really means it. He must help Americans to a new and more realistic concept of their national interest. He must explain that prudent expenditures on sustainable development overseas are not "foreign aid," but investments in survival.

Sir Shridath Ramphal, former Secretary-General of the Commonwealth, captured the meaning of the Earth Summit and the challenges of its aftermath when he spoke the following words at Rio: "Each of us—man, woman and child, rich and poor, of whatever faith, whatever race, whatever religion—must begin to take up our mutual dual citizenship. We must all of us belong, and have a sense of belonging, to two countries—our own and the planet."[2]

APPENDICES
EXCERPTS FROM AGENDA 21
Population
• • •

CHAPTER 5
DEMOGRAPHIC DYNAMICS AND SUSTAINABILITY

5.1. This chapter contains the following programme areas:

(a) Developing and disseminating knowledge concerning the links between demographic trends and factors and sustainable development;

(b) Formulating integrated national policies for environment and development, taking into account demographic trends and factors;

(c) Implementing integrated, environment and development programmes at the local level, taking into account demographic trends and factors.

• • •

B.   *Formulating integrated national policies for environment and development, taking into account demographic trends and factors*

Basis for action
5.16.   Existing plans for sustainable development have generally recognized demographic trends and factors as elements that have a critical influence on consumption patterns, production, lifestyles and long-term sustainability. But in future, more attention will have to be given to these issues in general policy formulation and the design of development plans. To do this, all countries will have to improve

51

their own capacities to assess the environment and development implications of their demographic trends and factors. They will also need to formulate and implement policies and action programmes where appropriate. Policies should be designed to address the consequences of population growth built into population momentum, while at the same time incorporating measures to bring about demographic transition.

• • •

Activities
5.23. An assessment should also be made of national population carrying capacity in the context of satisfaction of human needs and sustainable development, and special attention should be given to critical resources, such as water and land, and environmental factors, such as ecosystem health and biodiversity.

• • •

5.31. National population policy goals and programmes that are consistent with national environment and development plans for sustainability and in keeping with the freedom, dignity and personally held values of individuals should be established and implemented.

• • •

C. *Implementing integrated environment and development programmes at the local level, taking into account demographic trends and factors*

• • •

Activities

• • •

5.50. Governments should take active steps to implement, as a matter of urgency, in accordance with country-specific conditions and legal systems, measures to ensure that women and men have the same right to decide freely and responsibly on the number and spacing of their children, to have access to the information, education and means, as appropriate, to enable them to exercise this right in keeping with their freedom, dignity and personally held values taking into account ethical and cultural considerations.

5.51. Governments should take active steps to implement programmes to establish and strengthen preventive and curative health facilities that include women-centered, women-managed, safe and effective reproductive health care and affordable, accessible services, as appropriate, for the responsible planning of family size, in keeping with freedom, dignity and personally held values and taking into account ethical and cultural considerations.

• • •

Means of Implementation
(a) Financing and cost evaluation
5.57. The Conference secretariat has estimated the average total annual cost (1993-2000) of implementing the activities of this programme to be about $7 billion, including about $3.5 billion from the international community on grant or concessional terms. These are indicative and order of magnitude estimates only and have not been reviewed by Governments. Actual costs and financial terms, including any that are non-concessional, will depend upon, *inter alia,* the specific strategies and programmes Governments decide upon for implementation.

• • •

Financing

• • •

CHAPTER 33
FINANCIAL RESOURCES AND MECHANISMS

• • •

Means of Implementation
33.15. In general, the financing for the implemen-

tation of Agenda 21 will come from a country's own public and private sectors. For developing countries, particularly the least developed countries, ODA is a main source of external funding, and substantial new and additional funding for sustainable development and implementation of Agenda 21 will be required. Developed countries reaffirm their commitment to reach the accepted United Nations target of 0.7 per cent of GNP for ODA and, to the extent that they have not yet achieved that target, agree to augment their aid programmes in order to reach that target as soon as possible and to ensure a prompt and effective implementation of Agenda 21. Some countries agree or have agreed to reach the target by the year 2000. It was decided that the Commission on Sustainable Development would regularly review and monitor progress towards this target. This review process should systematically combine the monitoring of the implementation of Agenda 21 with a review of the financial resources available. Those countries which have already reached the target are to be commended and encouraged to continue to contribute to the common effort to make available the substantial additional resources that have to be mobilized. Other developed countries, in line with their support for reform efforts in developing countries, agree to make their best efforts to increase their level of ODA. In this context, the importance of equitable burden-sharing among developed countries is recognized. Other countries, including those undergoing the process of transition to a market economy, may voluntarily augment the contributions of the developed countries.

33.16. Funding for Agenda 21 and other outcomes of the Conference should be provided in a way which maximizes the availability of new and additional resources and which uses all available funding sources and mechanisms. These include, among others:

(a) *The multilateral development banks and funds:*
   (i) <u>International Development Association
(IDA)</u>. Among various issues and options that IDA
Deputies will examine in the forthcoming 10th
Replenishment, special consideration should be
given to the statement made by the President of the
International Bank for Reconstruction and Development at the Conference in plenary meeting in
order to help the poorest countries meet their
sustainable development objectives as contained in
Agenda 21.
   (ii) <u>Regional and subregional development
banks</u>. The regional and subregional development
banks and funds should play an increased and
more effective role in providing resources on
concessional or other favourable terms needed to
implement Agenda 21.
   (iii) <u>The Global Environment Facility</u>, managed
jointly by the World Bank, UNDP and UNEP, whose
additional grant and concessional funding is designed to achieve global environmental benefits
should cover the agreed incremental costs of relevant activities under Agenda 21, in particular for
developing countries. Therefore, it should be restructured so as to *inter alia*:
   Encourage universal participation;
   Have sufficient flexibility to expand its scope
and coverage to relevant programme areas of
Agenda 21, with global environmental benefits,
as agreed;
   Ensure a governance that is transparent
and democratic in nature, including in terms of
decision-making and operations, by guaranteeing a balanced and equitable representation of
the interests of developing countries, as well as
giving due weight to the funding efforts of donor
countries;
   Ensure new and additional financial resources on grant and concessional terms, in

particular to developing countries;

Ensure predictability in the flow of funds by contributions from developed countries, taking into account the importance of equitable burden-sharing;

Ensure access to and disbursement of the funds under mutually agreed criteria without introducing new forms of conditionality;

(b) *The relevant specialized agencies, other United Nations bodies and other international organizations,* which have designated roles to play in supporting national Governments in implementing Agenda 21;

(c) *Multilateral institutions for capacity-building and technical cooperation.* Necessary financial resources should be provided to UNDP to use its network of field offices and its broad mandate and experience in the field of technical cooperation for facilitating capacity-building at the country level, making full use of the expertise of the specialized agencies and other United Nations bodies within their respective areas of competence, in particular UNEP and including the multilateral and regional development banks;

(d) *Bilateral assistance programmes.* These will need to be strengthened in order to promote sustainable development;

(e) *Debt relief.* It is important to achieve durable solutions to the debt problems of low- and middle-income developing countries in order to provide them with the needed means for sustainable development. Measures to address the continuing debt problems of low- and middle-income countries should be kept under review. All creditors in the Paris Club should promptly implement the agreement of December 1991 to provide debt relief for the poorest heavily indebted countries pursuing structural adjustment; debt relief measures should be kept under review so as to address the continuing difficulties of those countries;

(f) *Private funding.* Voluntary contributions through non-governmental channels, which have been running at about 10 per cent of ODA, might be increased.

33.17. *Investment.* Mobilization of higher levels of foreign direct investment and technology transfers should be encouraged through national policies that promote investment and through joint ventures and other modalities.

33.18. *Innovative financing.* New ways of generating new public and private financial resources should be explored, in particular:

(a) Various forms of debt relief, apart from official or Paris Club debt, including greater use of debt swaps;

(b) The use of economic and fiscal incentives and mechanisms;

(c) The feasibility of tradeable permits;

(d) New schemes for fund-raising and voluntary contributions through private channels, including non-governmental organizations;

(e) The reallocation of resources presently committed to military purposes.

33.19. A supportive international and domestic economic climate conducive to sustained economic growth and development is important, particularly for developing countries, in order to achieve sustainability.

33.20. The secretariat of the Conference has estimated the average annual costs (1993-2000) of implementing in developing countries the activities in Agenda 21 to be over $600 billion, including about $125 billion on grant or concessional terms from the international community. These are indicative and order of magnitude estimates only, and have not been reviewed by Governments. Actual costs will depend upon, *inter alia,* the specific strategies and programmes Governments decide upon for implementation.

33.21. Developed countries and others in a position to do so should make initial financial commitments to give effect to the decisions of the Conference. They should report on such plans and commitments to the United Nations General Assembly in the Fall of 1992 at its forty-seventh session.

33.22. Developing countries should also begin to draw up national plans for sustainable development to give effect to the decisions of the Conference.

33.23. Review and monitoring of the financing of Agenda 21 is essential. Questions related to the effective follow-up of the Conference are discussed in chapter 38. It will be important to review on a regular basis the adequacy of funding and mechanisms, including efforts to reach agreed objectives of this chapter, including targets where applicable.

• • •

Institutions
• • •

CHAPTER 38
INTERNATIONAL INSTITUTIONAL ARRANGEMENTS

Institutional structure

A. *General Assembly*
38.9. The General Assembly, as the highest level intergovernmental mechanism, is the principal policy-making and appraisal organ on matters relating to the follow-up of the Conference. The Assembly would organize a regular review of the implementation of Agenda 21. In fulfilling this task, the Assembly could consider the timing, format and

organizational aspects of such a review. In particular, the Assembly could consider holding a special session no later than 1997 for the purposes of overall review and appraisal of Agenda 21, with adequate preparations at a high level.

B. *Economic and Social Council*
38.10. The Economic and Social Council, in the context of its Charter role *vis-à-vis* the General Assembly and the ongoing restructuring and revitalization of the United Nations in the economic, social and related fields, would assist the General Assembly through overseeing system-wide coordination, overview on the implementation of Agenda 21 and making recommendations in this regard. In addition, the Council would undertake the task of directing system-wide coordination and integration of environmental and developmental aspects in the United Nations policies and programmes and make appropriate recommendations to the General Assembly, specialized agencies concerned and Member States. Appropriate steps should be taken to obtain regular reports from specialized agencies on their plans and programmes related to the implementation of Agenda 21, pursuant to Article 64 of the Charter of the United Nations. The Economic and Social Council should organize a periodic review of the work of the Commission on Sustainable Development envisaged in paragraph 38.11, as well as of system-wide activities to integrate environment and development, making full use of its high-level and coordination segments.

C. *Intergovernmental mechanisms*
38.11. In order to ensure the effective follow-up of the Conference, as well as to enhance international cooperation and rationalize the intergovernmental decision-making capacity for the integration of environment and development issues and to exam-

ine the progress of the implementation of Agenda 21 at the national, regional and international levels, a high-level Commission on Sustainable Development should be established in accordance with Article 68 of the Charter of the United Nations. This Commission would report to the Economic and Social Council in the context of the Council's role under the Charter *vis-à-vis* the General Assembly. It would consist of representatives of States elected as members with due regard to equitable geographical distribution. Representatives of non-member States of the Commission would have observer status. The Commission should provide for the active involvement of organs, programmes and organizations of the United Nations system, international financial institutions and other relevant intergovernmental organizations, and encourage the participation of non-governmental organizations, including industry and the business and scientific communities. The first meeting of the commission should be convened no later than 1993. The Commission should be supported by the secretariat envisaged in paragraph 38.19. Meanwhile the Secretary-General of the United Nations is requested to ensure adequate interim administrative secretariat arrangements.

38.12. The General Assembly, at its forty-seventh session, should determine specific organizational modalities for the work of this Commission, such as its membership, its relationship with other intergovernmental United Nations bodies dealing with matters related to environment and development, and the frequency, duration and venue of its meetings. These modalities should take into account the ongoing process of revitalization and restructuring of the work of the United Nations in the economic, social and related fields, in particular measures recommended by the General Assembly in resolutions 45/264 of 13 May 1991 and 46/235 of 13 April 1992 and other relevant Assembly resolutions. In this respect, the Secretary-General of the United Nations, with the assistance of the Secretary-General of the United Nations Conference on Environment and Development, is requested to prepare for the Assembly a report with appropriate recommendations and proposals.

D. Intergovernmental functions

38.13. The Commission on Sustainable Development should have the following functions:

(a) To monitor progress in the implementation of Agenda 21 and activities related to the integration of environmental and developmental goals throughout the United Nations system through analysis and evaluation of reports from all relevant organs, organizations, programmes and institutions of the United Nations system dealing with various issues of environment and development, including those related to finance;

(b) To consider information provided by Governments, including, for example, information in the form of periodic communications or national reports regarding the activities they undertake to implement Agenda 21, the problems they face, such as problems related to financial resources and technology transfer, and other environment and development issues they find relevant.

(c) To review the progress in the implementation of the commitments contained in Agenda 21, including those related to provision of financial resources and transfer of technology;

(d) To receive and analyse relevant input from competent non-governmental organizations, including the scientific and the private sector, in the context of the overall implementation of Agenda 21;

(e) To enhance the dialogue within the framework of the United Nations with non-governmental organizations and the independent sector as well as other entities outside the United Nations system;

(f) To consider, where appropriate, information regarding the progress made in the implementation of environmental conventions, which could be made available by the relevant Conferences of Parties.

(g) To provide appropriate recommendations to the General Assembly on the basis of an integrated consideration of the reports and issues related to the implementation of Agenda 21;

(h) To consider, at an appropriate time, the results of the review to be conducted expeditiously by the Secretary-General of all recommendations of the Conference for capacity-building programmes, information networks, task forces and other mechanisms to support the integration of environment and development at regional and subregional levels.

38.14. Within the intergovernmental framework, consideration should be given to allow non-governmental organizations including those related to major groups, particularly women's groups, committed to the implementation of Agenda 21 to have relevant information available to them including information, reports and other data produced within the United Nations system.

E. *The Secretary-General*
38.15. Strong and effective leadership on the part of the Secretary-General is crucial, since he/she would be the focal point of the institutional arrangements within the United Nations system for the successful follow-up to the Conference and for the implementation of Agenda 21.

F. *High-level inter-agency coordination mechanism*
38.16. Agenda 21, as the basis for action by the international community to integrate environment

and development, should provide the principal framework for coordination of relevant activities within the United Nations system. To ensure effective monitoring, coordination and supervision of the involvement of the United Nations system in the follow-up to the Conference, there is a need for a coordination mechanism under the direct leadership of the Secretary-General.

38.17. This task should be given to the Administrative Committee on Coordination (ACC) headed by the Secretary-General. ACC would thus provide a vital link and interface between the multilateral financial institutions and other United Nations bodies at the highest administrative level. The Secretary-General should continue to revitalize the functioning of the Committee. All heads of agencies and institutions of the United Nations system shall be expected to cooperate with the Secretary-General fully in order to make ACC work effectively in fulfilling its crucial role and ensure successful implementation of Agenda 21. ACC should consider establishing a special task force, subcommittee or sustainable development board, taking into account the experience of the Designated Officials for Environmental Matters (DOEM) and the Committee of International Development Institutions on Environment (CIDIE), as well as the respective roles of UNEP and UNDP. Its report should be submitted to the relevant intergovernmental bodies.

G. *High-level advisory body*
38.18. Intergovernmental bodies, the Secretary-General and the United Nations system as a whole may also benefit from the expertise of a high-level advisory board consisting of eminent persons knowledgeable about environment and development, including relevant sciences, appointed by the Secretary-General in their personal capacity. In this regard, the Secretary-General should make appro-

priate recommendations to the General Assembly at its forty-seventh session.

H. *Secretariat support structure*

38.19. A highly qualified and competent secretariat support structure drawing, *inter alia*, on the expertise gained in the Conference preparatory process is essential for the follow-up to the Conference and the implementation of Agenda 21. This secretariat support structure should provide support to the work of both intergovernmental and inter-agency coordination mechanisms. Concrete organizational decisions fall within the competence of the Secretary-General as the chief administrative officer of the Organization, who is requested to report on the provisions to be made, covering staffing implications, as soon as practicable, taking into account gender balance as defined in Article 8 of the United Nations Charter, and the need for the best use of existing resources in the context of current and ongoing restructuring of the United Nations Secretariat.

I. *Organs, programmes and organizations of the United Nations System*

38.20. In the follow-up to the Conference, in particular implementation of Agenda 21, all relevant organs, programmes and organizations of the United Nations system will have an important role within their respective areas of expertise and mandates in supporting and supplementing national efforts. Coordination and mutual complementarity of their efforts to promote integration of environment and development can be enhanced through countries encouraging to maintain consistent positions in the various governing bodies.

1. *United Nations Environment Programme*

38.21. In the follow-up to the Conference, there will be a need for an enhanced and strengthened role of

UNEP and its Governing Council. The Governing Council should within its mandate continue to play its role with regard to policy guidance and coordination in the field of the environment, taking into account the development perspective.

38.22. Priority areas on which UNEP should concentrate include the following:

(a) Strengthening its catalytic role in stimulating and promoting environmental activities and considerations throughout the United Nations system;

(b) Promoting international cooperation in the field of environment and recommending, as appropriate, policies to this end;

(c) Developing and promoting the use of techniques such as natural resource accounting and environmental economies;

(d) Environmental monitoring and assessment, both through improved participation by the United Nations system agencies in the Earthwatch programme and expanded relations with private scientific and non-governmental research institutes; strengthening and making operational its early-warning function;

(e) Coordination and promotion of relevant scientific research with a view to providing a consolidated basis for decision-making;

(f) Dissemination of environmental information and date to Governments and to organs, programmes and organizations of the United Nations system;

(g) Raising general awareness and action in the area of environmental protection through collaboration with the general public, non-governmental entities and intergovernmental institutions;

(h) Further development of international environmental law, in particular conventions and guidelines, promotion of its implementation, and coordinating functions arising from an increasing number of international legal agreements, *inter alia*, the functioning of the secretariats of the Conventions, taking into account the need for the most efficient use of resources, including possible co-location of secretariats established in the future;

(i) Further development and promotion of the widest possible use of environmental impact assessments, including activities carried out under the auspices of United Nations specialized agencies, and in connection with every significant economic development project or activity;

(j) Facilitation of information exchange on environmentally sound technologies, including legal aspects, and provision of training;

(k) Promotion of subregional and regional co-operation and support to relevant initiatives and programmes for environmental protection, including playing a major contributing and coordinating role in the regional mechanisms in the field of environment identified for the follow-up to the Conference;

(l) Provision of technical, legal and institutional advice to Governments, upon request, in establishing and enhancing their national legal and institutional frameworks, in particular, in cooperation with UNDP capacity-building efforts;

(m) Support to Governments, upon request, and development agencies and organs in the integration of environmental aspects into their development policies and programmes, in particular through provision of environmental, technical and policy advice during programme formulation and implementation;

(n) Further developing assessment and assistance in cases of environmental emergencies.

38.23. In order for UNEP to perform all of these functions, while retaining its role as the principal body within the United Nations system in the field of environment and taking into account the development aspects of environmental questions, it would require access to greater expertise and provision of adequate financial resources and it would require closer cooperation and collaboration with development organs and other relevant organs of the United Nations system. Furthermore, the regional offices of UNEP should be strengthened without weakening its Headquarters in Nairobi, and UNEP should take steps to reinforce and intensity its liaison and interaction with UNDP and the World Bank.

2. *United Nations Development Programme*
38.24. UNDP, like UNEP, also has a crucial role in the follow-up to the United Nations Conference on Environment and Development. Through its network of field offices it would foster the United Nations system's collective thrust in support of the implementation of Agenda 21, at the country, regional, interregional and global levels, drawing on the expertise of the specialized agencies and other United Nations organizations and bodies involved in operational activities. The role of the resident representative/resident coordinator of UNDP needs to be strengthened in order to coordinate the field-level activities of the United Nations operational activities.

38.25. Its role would include the following:

(a) Acting as the lead agency in organizing United Nations system efforts towards capacity-building at the local, national and regional levels;

(b) Mobilizing donor resources on behalf of Governments for capacity-building in recipient countries and, where appropriate, through the use of the UNDP donor round-table mechanisms;

(c) Strengthening its own programmes in support of follow-up to the Conference without prejudice to the Fifth Programme Cycle;

(d) Assisting recipient countries upon request,

in the establishing and strengthening of national coordination mechanisms and networks related to activities for the follow-up of the Conference;

(e) Assisting recipient countries upon request, in coordinating the mobilization of domestic financial resources;

(f) Promoting and strengthening the role and involvement of women, youth and other major groups, in recipient countries in the implementation of Agenda 21.

3. United Nations Conference on Trade and Development

38.26. The United Nations Conference on Trade and Development should play an important role in the implementation of Agenda 21 as extended at the eighth session of the Conference, taking into account the importance of the interrelationships between development, international trade and the environment and in accordance with its mandate in the area of sustainable development.

4. United Nations Sudano-Sahelian Office

38.27. The role of the United Nations Sudano-Sahelian Office (UNSO), with added resources that may become available, operating under the umbrella of UNDP and with the support of UNEP, should be strengthened so that this body can assume an appropriate major advisory role and participate effectively in the implementation of Agenda 21 provisions related to combating drought and desertification as well as land resource management. In this context, the experience gained could be used by all other countries affected by drought and desertification, in particular those in Africa, with special attention to countries most affected or classified as least developed countries.

5. United Nations specialized agencies and related

organizations and other relevant intergovernmental organizations

38.28. All United Nations specialized agencies, related organizations and other relevant intergovernmental organizations within their respective fields of competence have an important role to play in the implementation of relevant parts of Agenda 21 and other decisions of the Conference. Their governing bodies may consider ways of strengthening and adjusting activities and programmes in line with Agenda 21, in particular, regarding projects for promoting sustainable development. Furthermore, they may consider establishing special arrangements with donors and financial institutions for project implementation that may require additional resources.

J. Regional and subregional cooperation and implementation

38.29. Regional and subregional cooperation will be an important part of the outcome of the Conference. The regional commissions, regional development banks and regional economic and technical cooperation organizations, within their respective agreed mandates, can contribute to this process by:

(a) Promoting regional and subregional capacity-building;

(b) Promoting the integration of environmental concerns in regional and subregional development policies;

(c) Promoting regional and subregional cooperation, where appropriate, regarding transboundary issues related to sustainable development.

38.30. The regional commissions, as appropriate, should play a leading role in coordinating regional and subregional activities by sectoral and other United Nations bodies and shall assist countries in achieving sustainable development. The commissions and regional programmes within the United

Nations system, as well as other regional organizations, should review the need for modification of ongoing activities, as appropriate, in light of Agenda 21.

38.31. There must be active cooperation and collaboration among the regional commissions and other relevant organizations, regional development banks, non-governmental organizations and other institutions at the regional level. UNEP and UNDP, together with the regional commissions, would have a crucial role to play, especially in providing the necessary assistance, with particular emphasis on building and strengthening the national capacity of Member States.

38.32. There is a need for closer cooperation between UNEP and UNDP, together with other relevant institutions, in the implementation of projects to halt environmental degradation or its impact and to support training programmes in environmental planning and management for sustainable development at the regional level.

38.33. Regional intergovernmental technical and economic organizations have an important role to play in helping Governments to take coordinated action in solving environment issues of regional significance.

38.34. Regional and subregional organizations should play a major role in the implementation of the provisions of Agenda 21 related to combating drought and desertification. UNEP, UNDP and UNSO should assist and cooperate with those relevant organizations.

38.35. Cooperation between regional and subregional organizations and relevant organizations of the United Nations system should be encouraged, where appropriate, in other sectoral areas.

K. *National implementation*

38.36. States have an important role to play in the follow-up of the Conference and the implementation of Agenda 21. National level efforts should be undertaken by all countries in an integrated manner so that both environment and development concerns can be dealt with in a coherent manner. 38.37. Policy decisions and activities at the national level, tailored to support and implement Agenda 21, should be supported by the United Nations system upon request. 38.38. Furthermore, States could consider the preparation of national reports. In this context, the organs of the United Nations system should, upon request, assist countries, in particular developing countries. Countries could also consider the preparation of national action plans for the implementation of Agenda 21. 38.39. Existing assistance consortia, consultative groups and roundtables should make greater efforts to integrate environmental considerations and related development objectives into their development assistance strategies, and consider reorienting and appropriately adjusting their memberships and operations to facilitate this process and better support national efforts to integrate environment and development. 38.40 States may wish to consider setting up a national coordination structure responsible for the follow-up of Agenda 21. Within this structure, which would benefit from the expertise of non-governmental organizations, submissions and other relevant information could be made to the United Nations.

L.Cooperation between United Nations bodies and international financial organizations
38.41. The success of the follow-up to the Conference is dependent upon an effective link between substantive action and financial support, and this requires close and effective cooperation between United Nations bodies and the multilateral finan-

cial organizations. The Secretary-General and heads of United Nations programmes, organizations and the multilateral financial organizations have a special responsibility in forging such a cooperation, not only through the United Nations high-level coordination mechanism (Administrative Committee on Coordination) but also at regional and national levels. In particular, representatives of multilateral financial institutions and mechanisms, as well as the International Fund for Agricultural Development (IFAD), should actively be associated with deliberations of the intergovernmental structure responsible for the follow-up to Agenda 21.

M. *Non-governmental organizations*
38.42. Non-governmental organizations and major groups are important partners in the implementation of Agenda 21. Relevant non-governmental organizations, including the scientific community, the private sector, women's groups etc., should be given opportunities to make their contributions and establish appropriate relationships with the United Nations system. Support should be provided for developing countries' non-governmental organizations and their self-organized networks.
38.43. The United Nations system, including international finance and development agencies, and all intergovernmental organizations and forums should, in consultation with non-governmental organizations, take measures to:

(a) Design open and effective means to achieve the participation of non-governmental organizations, including those related to major groups, in the process established to review and evaluate the implementation of Agenda 21 at all levels and promote their contribution to it;

(b) Take into account the findings of review systems and evaluation processes of non-governmental organizations in relevant reports of the

Secretary-General to the General Assembly and all pertinent United Nations agencies and intergovernmental organizations and forums concerning implementation of Agenda 21 in accordance with its review process.

38.44. Procedures should be established for an expanded role for non-governmental organizations, including those related to major groups, with accreditation based on the procedures used in the Conference. Such organizations should have access to reports and other information produced by the United Nations system. The General Assembly, at an early stage, should examine ways of enhancing the involvement of non-governmental organizations within the United Nations system in relation to the follow-up process of the Conference.

38.45. The Conference takes note of other institutional initiatives for the implementation of Agenda 21, such as the proposal to establish a non-governmental Earth Council and the proposal to appoint a guardian for future generations as well as other initiatives by local governments and business sectors.

• • •

FRAMEWORK CONVENTION
ON CLIMATE CHANGE

ARTICLE 2
OBJECTIVE

The ultimate objective of this Convention and any related legal instruments that the Conference of the Parties may adopt is to achieve, in accordance with the relevant provisions of the Convention, stabilization of greenhouse gas concentrations in the atmosphere at a level that would prevent dangerous anthropogenic interference with the climate system. Such a level should be achieved within a time frame sufficient to allow ecosystems to adapt naturally to climate change, to ensure that food production is not threatened and to enable economic development to proceed in a sustainable manner.

ARTICLE 3
PRINCIPLES

In their actions to achieve the objective of the Convention and to implement its provisions, the Parties shall be guided, *inter alia*, by the following:

1.   The Parties should protect the climate system for the benefit of present and future generations of humankind, on the basis of equity and in accordance with their common but differentiated responsibilities and respective capabilities. Accord-

ingly, the developed country Parties should take the lead in combating climate change and the adverse effects thereof.

2. The specific needs and special circumstances of developing country Parties, especially those that are particularly vulnerable to the adverse effects of climate change, and of those Parties, especially developing country Parties, that would have to bear a disproportionate or abnormal burden under the Convention, should be given full consideration.

3. The Parties should take precautionary measures to anticipate, prevent or minimize the causes of climate change and mitigate its adverse effects. Where there are threats of serious or irreversible damage, lack of full scientific certainty should not be used as a reason for postponing such measures, taking into account that policies and measures to deal with climate change should be cost-effective so as to ensure global benefits at the lowest possible cost. To achieve this, such policies and measures should take into account different socio-economic contexts, be comprehensive, cover all relevant sources, sinks and reseviors of greenhouse gases and adaptation, and comprise all economic sectors. Efforts to address climate change may be carried out cooperatively by interested Parties.

4. The Parties have a right to, and should, promote sustainable development. Policies and measures to protect the climate system against human-induced change should be appropriate for the specific conditions of each Party and should be integrated with national development programmes, taking into account that economic development is essential for adopting measures to address climate change.

5. The Parties should cooperate to promote a supportive and open international economic system that would lead to sustainable economic growth and development in all Parties, particularly devel-

oping country Parties, thus enabling them better to address the problems of climate change. Measures taken to combat climate change, including unilateral ones, should not constitute a means of arbitrary or unjustifiable discrimination or a disguised restriction on international trade.

ARTICLE 4
COMMITMENTS

1.   All Parties, taking into account their common but differentiated responsibilities and their specific national and regional development priorities, objectives and circumstances, shall:

(a) Develop, periodically update, publish and make available to the Conference of the Parties, in accordance with Article 12, national inventories of anthropogenic emissions by sources and removals by sinks of all greenhouse gases not controlled by the Montreal Protocol, using comparable methodologies to be agreed upon by the Conference of the Parties;

(b) Formulate, implement, publish and regularly update national and, where appropriate, regional programmes containing measures to mitigate climate change by addressing anthropogenic emissions by sources and removals by sinks of all greenhouse gases not controlled by the Montreal Protocol, and measures to facilitate adequate adaptation to climate change;

(c) Promote and cooperate in the development, application and diffusion, including transfer, of technologies, practices and processes that control, reduce or prevent anthropogenic emissions of greenhouse gases not controlled by the Montreal Protocol in all relevant sectors, including the energy, transport, industry, agriculture, forestry and waste management sectors;

(d) Promote sustainable management, and promote and cooperate in the conservation and enhancement, as appropriate, of sinks and reservoirs of all greenhouse gases not controlled by the Montreal Protocol, including biomass, forests and oceans as well as other terrestrial, coastal and marine ecosystems;

(e) Cooperate in preparing for adaptation to the impacts of climate change; develop and elaborate appropriate and integrated plans for coastal zone management, water resources and agriculture, and for the protection and rehabilitation of areas, particularly in Africa, affected by drought and desertification, as well as floods.

(f) Take climate change considerations into account, to the extent feasible, in their relevant social, economic and environmental policies and actions, and employ appropriate methods, for example impact assessments, formulated and determined nationally, with a view to minimizing adverse effects on the economy, on public health and on the quality of the environment, of projects or measures undertaken by them to mitigate or adapt to climate change;

(g) Promote and cooperate in scientific, technological, technical, socio-economic and other research, systematic observation and development of data archives related to the climate system and intended to further the understanding and to reduce or eliminate the remaining uncertainties regarding the causes, effects, magnitude and timing of climate change and the economic and social consequences of various response strategies;

(h) Promote and cooperate in the full, open and prompt exchange of relevant scientific, technological, technical, socio-economic and legal information related to the climate system and climate change, and to the economic and social consequences of various response strategies;

(i) Promote and cooperate in education, training and public awareness related to climate change and encourage the widest participation in this process, including that of non-governmental organizations; and

(j) Communicate to the Conference of the Parties information related to implementation, in accordance with Article 12.

2. The developed country Parties and other Parties included in annex I commit themselves specifically as provided for in the following:

(a) Each of these Parties shall adopt national policies and take corresponding measures on the mitigation of climate change, by limiting its anthropogenic emissions of greenhouse gases and protecting and enhancing its greenhouse gas sinks and resevoirs. These policies and measures will demonstrate that developed countries are taking the lead in modifying longer-term trends in anthropogenic emissions consistent with the objective of the Convention, recognizing that the return by the end of the present decade to earlier levels of anthropogenic emissions of carbon dioxide and other greenhouse gases not controlled by the Montreal Protocol would contribute to such modification, and taking into account the differences in these Parties' starting points and approaches, economic structures and resource bases, the need to maintain strong and sustainable economic growth, available technologies and other individual circumstances, as well as the need for equitable and appropriate contributions by each of these Parties to the global effort regarding that objective. These Parties may implement such policies and measures jointly with other Parties and may assist other Parties in contributing to the achievement of the objective of the Convention and, in particular, that of this subparagraph;

(b) In order to promote progress to this end,

each of these Parties shall communicate, within six months of the entry into force of the Convention for it and periodically thereafter, and in accordance with Article 12, detailed information on its policies and measures referred to in subparagraph (a) above, as well as on its resulting projected anthropogenic emissions by sources and removals by sinks of greenhouse gases not controlled by the Montreal Protocol for the period referred to in subparagraph (a), with the aim of returning individually or jointly to their 1990 levels of these anthropogenic emissions of carbon dioxide and other greenhouse gases not controlled by the Montreal Protocol. This information will be reviewed by the Conference of the Parties, at its first session and periodically thereafter, in accordance with Article 7;

(c) Calculations of emission by sources and removals by sinks of greenhouse gases for the purposes of subparagraph (b) above should take into account the best available scientific knowledge, including of the effective capacity of sinks and the respective contributions of such gases to climate change. The Conference of the Parties shall consider and agree on methodologies for these calculations at its first session and review them regularly thereafter;

(d) The Conference of the Parties shall, at its first session, review the adequacy of subparagraphs (a) and (b) above. Such review shall be carried out in the light of the best available scientific information and assessment on climate change and its impacts, as well as relevant technical, social and economic information. Based on this review, the Conference of the Parties shall take appropriate action, which may include the adoption of amendments to the commitments in subparagraphs (a) and (b) above. The Conference of the Parties, at its first session, shall also take decisions regarding criteria for joint implementation as indicated in subparagraph (a) above. A second review of subparagraphs (a) and (b) shall take place not later than 31 December 1998, and thereafter at regular intervals determined by the Conference of the Parties, until the objective of the Convention is met;

(e) Each of these Parties shall:

(i) coordinate as appropriate with other such Parties, relevant economic and administrative instruments developed to achieve the objective of the convention; and

(ii) identify and periodically review is own policies and practices which encourage activities that lead to greater levels of anthropogenic emissions of greenhouse gases not controlled by the Montreal Protocol than would otherwise occur;

(f) The Conference of the Parties shall review, not later than 31 December 1998, available information with a view to taking decisions regarding such amendments to the lists in annexes I and II as may be appropriate, with the approval of the Party concerned;

(g) Any Party not included in annex I may, in its instrument of ratification, acceptance, approval or accession, or at any time thereafter, notify the Depositary that it intends to be bound by subparagraphs (a) and (b) above. The Depositary shall inform the other signatories and Parties of any such notification.

3. The developed country Parties and other developed Parties included in annex II shall provide new and additional financial resources to meet the agreed full costs incurred by developing country Parties in complying with their obligations under Article 12, paragraph 1. They shall also provide such financial resources, including for the transfer of technology, needed by the developing country Parties to meet the agreed full incremental costs of implementing measures that are covered by para-

graph 1 of this Article and that are agreed between a developing country Party and the international entity or entities referred to in Article 11, in accordance with that Article. The implementation of these commitments shall take into account the need for adequacy and the predictability in the flow of funds and the importance of appropriate burden sharing among the developed country Parties.

4. The developed country Parties and other developed Parties included in annex II shall also assist the developing country Parties that are particularly vulnerable to the adverse effects of climate change in meeting costs of adaptation to those adverse effects.

5. The developed country Parties and other developed Parties included in annex II shall take all practicable steps to promote, facilitate and finance, as appropriate, the transfer of, or access to, environmentally sound technologies and know-how to other Parties, particularly developing country Parties, to enable them to implement the provisions of the Convention. In this process, the developed country Parties shall support the development and enhancement of endogenous capacities and technologies of developing country Parties. Other Parties and organizations in a position to do so may also assist in facilitating the transfer of such technologies.

6. In the implementation of their commitments under paragraph 2 above, a certain degree of flexibility shall be allowed by the Conference of the Parties to the Parties included in annex I undergoing the process of transition to a market economy, in order to enhance the ability of these Parties to address climate change, including with regard to the historical level of anthropogenic emissions of greenhouse gases not controlled by the Montreal Protocol chosen as a reference.

7. The extent to which developing country Parties

will effectively implement their commitments under the Convention will depend on the effective implementation by developed country Parties of their commitments under the Convention related to financial resources and transfer of technology and will take fully into account that economic and social development and poverty eradication are the first and overriding priorities of the developing country Parties.

8. In the implementation of the commitments in this Article, the Parties shall give full consideration to what actions are necessary under the Convention, including actions related to funding, insurance and the transfer of technology, to meet the specific needs and concerns of developing country Parties arising from the adverse effects of climate change and/or the impact of the implementation of response measures, especially on:

(a) Small island countries;

(b) Countries with low-lying coastal areas;

(c) Countries with arid and semi-arid areas, forested areas and areas liable to forest decay;

(d) Countries with areas prone to natural disasters;

(e) Countries with areas liable to drought and desertification;

(f) Countries with areas of high urban atmospheric pollution;

(g) Countries with areas with fragile ecosystems, including mountainous ecosystems;

(h) Countries whose economies are highly dependent on income generated from the production, processing and export, and/or on consumption of fossil fuels and associated energy-intensive products; and

(i) Land-locked and transit countries.

Further, the Conference of the Parties may take actions, as appropriate, with respect to this paragraph.

9. The Parties shall take full account of the specific needs and special situations of the least developed countries in their actions with regard to funding and transfer of technology.

10. The Parties shall, in accordance with Article 10, take into consideration in the implementation of the commitments of the Convention the situation of Parties, particularly developing country Parties, with economies that are vulnerable to the adverse effects of the implementation of measures to respond to climate change. This applies notably to Parties with economies that are highly dependent on income generated from the production, processing and export, and/or consumption of fossil fuels and associated energy-intensive products and/or the use of fossil fuels for which such parties have serious difficulties in switching to alternatives.

• • •

ARTICLE 21
INTERIM ARRANGEMENTS

• • •

3. The Global Environment Facility of the United Nations Development Programme, the United Nations Environment Programme and the International Bank for Reconstruction and Development shall be the international entity entrusted with the operation of the financial mechanism referred to in Article 11 on an interim basis. In this connection, the Global Environment Facility should be appropriately restructured and its membership made universal to enable it to fulfil the requirements of Article 11.

• • •

CONVENTION ON BIOLOGICAL DIVERSITY

ARTICLE 8
IN-SITU CONSERVATION

Each Contracting Party shall, as far as possible and as appropriate:

(a) Establish a system of protected areas or areas where special measures need to be taken to conserve biological diversity;

(b) Develop, where necessary, guidelines for the selection, establishment and management of protected areas or areas where special measures need to be taken to conserve biological diversity;

(c) Regulate or manage biological resources important for the conservation of biological diversity whether within or outside protected areas, with a view to ensuring their conservation and sustainable use;

(d) Promote the protection of ecosystems, natural habitats and the maintenance of viable populations of species in natural surroundings;

(e) Promote environmentally sound and sustainable development in areas adjacent to protected areas with a view to furthering protection of these areas;

(f) Rehabilitate and restore degraded ecosystems and promote the recovery of threatened species, *inter alia*, through the development and implementation of plans or other management strategies;

(g) Establish or maintain means to regulate, manage or control the risks associated with the use and release of living modified organisms resulting from biotechnology which are likely to have adverse environmental impacts that could affect the conservation and sustainable use of biological diversity, taking also into account the risks to human health;

(h) Prevent the introduction of, control or eradicate those alien species which threaten ecosystems, habitats or species;

(i) Endeavor to provide the conditions needed for compatibility between present uses and the conservation of biological diversity and the sustainable use of its components;

(j) Subject to its national legislation, respect, preserve and maintain knowledge, innovations and practices of indigenous and local communities embodying traditional lifestyles relevant for the conservation and sustainable use of biological diversity and promote their wider application with the approval and involvement of the holders of such knowledge, innovations and practices and encourage the equitable sharing of the benefits arising from the utilization of such knowledge, innovations and practices;

(k) Develop or maintain necessary legislation and/or other regulatory provisions for the protection of threatened species and populations;

(l) Where a significant adverse effect on biological diversity has been determined pursuant to Article 7, regulate or manage the relevant processes and categories of activities; and

(m)   Cooperate in providing financial and other support for in-situ conservation outlined in subparagraphs (a) to (l) above, particularly to developing countries.

ARTICLE 16
ACCESS TO AND TRANSFER OF TECHNOLOGY

1. Each Contracting Party, recognizing that technology includes biotechnology, and that both access to and transfer of technology among Contracting Parties are essential elements for the attainment of the objectives of this Convention, undertakes subject to the provisions of this Article to provide and/or facilitate access for and transfer to other Contracting Parties of technologies that are relevant to the conservation and sustainable use of biological diversity or make use of genetic resources and do not cause significant damage to the environment.

2. Access to and transfer of technology referred to in paragraph 1 above to developing countries shall be provided and/or facilitated under fair and most favourable terms, including on concessional and preferential terms where mutually agreed, and, where necessary, in accordance with the financial mechanism established by Articles 20 and 21. In the case of technology subject to patents and other intellectual property rights, such access and transfer shall be provided on terms which recognize and are consistent with the adequate and effective protection of intellectual property rights. The application of this paragraph shall be consistent with paragraphs 3, 4 and 5 below.

3. Each Contracting Party shall take legislative, administrative or policy measures, as appropriate, with the aim that Contracting Parties, in particular those that are developing countries, which provide genetic resources are provided access to and transfer of technology which makes use of those resources, on mutually agreed terms, including technology protected by patents and other intellectual

property rights, where necessary, through the provisions of Articles 20 and 21 and in accordance with international law and consistent with paragraphs 4 and 5 below.

4. Each Contracting Party shall take legislative, administrative or policy measures, as appropriate, with the aim that the private sector facilitates access to, joint development and transfer of technology referred to in paragraph 1 above for the benefit of both governmental institutions and the private sector of developing countries and in this regard shall abide by the obligations included in paragraphs 1, 2 and 3 above.

5. The Contracting Parties, recognizing that patents and other intellectual property rights may have an influence on the implementation of this Convention, shall cooperate in this regard subject to national legislation and international law in order to ensure that such rights are supportive of and do not run counter to its objectives.

• • •

ARTICLE 21
FINANCIAL MECHANISM

1. There shall be a mechanism for the provision of financial resources to developing country Parties for purposes of this Convention on a grant or concessional basis the essential elements of which are described in this Article. The mechanism shall function under the authority and guidance of, and be accountable to, the Conference of the Parties for purposes of this Convention. The operations of the mechanism shall be carried out by such institutional structure as may be decided upon by the Conference of the Parties at its first meeting. For purposes of this Convention, the Conference of the Parties shall determine the policy, strategy, programme priorities and eligibility criteria relating

to the access to and utilization of such resources. The contributions shall be such as to take into account the need for predictability, adequacy and timely flow of funds referred to in Article 20 in accordance with the amount of resources needed to be decided periodically by the Conference of the Parties and the importance of burden-sharing among the contributing Parties included in the list referred to in Article 20, paragraph 2. Voluntary contributions may also be made by the developed country Parties and by other countries and sources. The mechanism shall operate within a democratic and transparent system of governance.

2.   Pursuant to the objectives of this Convention, the Conference of the Parties shall at its first meeting determine the policy, strategy and programme priorities, as well as detailed criteria and guidelines for eligibility for access to and utilization of the financial resources including monitoring and evaluation on a regular basis of such utilization. The Conference of the Parties shall decide on the arrangements to give effect to paragraph 1 above after consultation with the institutional structure entrusted with the operation of the financial mechanism.

3.   The Conference of the Parties shall review the effectiveness of the mechanism established under this Article, including the criteria and guidelines referred to in paragraph 2 above, not less than two years after the entry into force of this Convention and thereafter on a regular basis. Based on such review, it shall take appropriate action to improve the effectiveness of the mechanism if necessary.

4.   The Contracting Parties shall consider strengthening existing financial institutions to provide financial resources for the conservation and sustainable use of biological diversity.

NOTES

Chapter 2

[1] The Reilly memorandum, circulated to EPA employees in mid-July, was reported in Keith Schneider, "Bush Aide Assails U.S. Preparations for Earth Summit," *The New York Times*, August 1, 1992, p. 1.

Chapter 3

[1] "Summit to Save the Earth," *Time*, June 1, 1992, p. 54.

[2] Statement by Ambassador George Bush at the Dallas Council on World Affairs, US Mission to the UN Press Release USUN-74(71), May 28, 1971.

Chapter 7

[1] Carnegie Endowment for International Peace, *Changing our Ways: America and the New World* (Washington, D.C.: July, 1992.).

[2] "Sir Shridath Ramphal Addresses Riocentro Group," *Earth Summit Times* (the NGO newspaper published during the conference), June 6, 1992.

ABOUT THE AUTHOR

Richard N. Gardner is the Henry L. Moses Professor of Law and International Organization at Columbia University and Of Counsel to the law firm of Coudert Brothers. He served as U.S. Ambassador to Italy from 1977 to 1981 and as Deputy Assistant Secretary of State for International Organization Affairs from 1961 to 1965. He was a Special Advisor to the UN at the Earth Summit in Rio, as he was twenty years earlier at the Stockholm Conference on the Human Environment.

Ambassador Gardner holds a B.A. degree in Economics from Harvard College, a Doctor of Jurisprudence from Yale Law School, and a Doctor of Philosophy in Economics from Oxford University, where he studied as a Rhodes Scholar. He is author of four books, including *Sterling-Dollar Diplomacy: The Origins and the Prospects of Our International Economic Order,* and *In Pursuit of World Order: U.S. Foreign Policy and International Organization.*